Dani Binns
Clever Chef

Written by Lisa Rajan

Illustrated by Alessia Trunfio

Collins

Chapter 1

Dani Binns finished chatting to her sister
Tara and went into the spare bedroom, looking
for the old toy box. There it was! She opened
the lid and looked inside. Every time she took
something from the box, it gave her a job to do
and sent her off on an adventure.

She picked out a pack of chalk pens.

Maybe I'll be an artist? she thought.

Her hand began to tingle. The tingling spread up her arm and around her whole body. Then she began spinning and tumbling through space and time …

Chapter 2

When the spinning stopped, Dani found herself in the bustling kitchen of a restaurant. All around her were busy chefs – chopping, peeling, slicing, preparing and cooking. It was hot and extremely noisy.

"Ah! You're here," said a boy in a tall hat. "I'm Tai and this is Asha. We're the head chefs. The restaurant is really busy today. You'll be helping Izzy, the sauce chef."

"You won't need chalk pens," smiled Asha. "The menu blackboard is in the restaurant, not the kitchen! You'll need *these*." Asha held out a hat and an apron.

Izzy had nearly finished making three sauces.

"One is salad dressing, for the starter. One is curry sauce, for the main course. That one is toffee syrup, for the pudding," Izzy told Dani.

They all look the same, thought Dani.

"Can you smell burning?" Izzy asked Dani, sniffing the air and glancing around. "You finish the sauces, while I investigate. Lemon juice in … *er* … that one. Chilli in … *umm* … that one and sugar in that one."

Dani followed Izzy's instructions. Then she poured the sauces on to the plates and the waiter took them out to the customers.

Two minutes later, the waiter was back.

"What's wrong?" Asha asked.

"The customers are complaining. Three have stormed out! The salad tastes sweet, the curry tastes sour and the toffee pudding tastes spicy. What's going on?" the waiter asked.

Dani gulped.

"Oh dear. I got distracted by this food burning and must have got the pans mixed up when I told Dani which sauce was which. Sorry," Izzy apologised.

"We'll have to throw the sauces away and start again," moaned Tai. "What a waste!"

Chapter 3

Izzy started again. Dani helped gather the ingredients they needed for all three sauces. They had to work fast. The customers would be getting hungry and impatient.

Izzy grabbed the chilli. She was about to add it to one of the saucepans but paused ...

"What's wrong?" asked Dani.

"I can't remember if I've added this already … and to which pan!" Izzy replied.

Dani saw Tai putting the new meals on to plates. He would be heading over for the sauces soon.

How can I solve this problem? wondered Dani.

Dani remembered her chalk pens and had
an idea. She took out the green, red and
brown pens.

She drew three circles on the worktop
next to the hob, in the same positions as
the three saucepans. She wrote "Dressing"
in the green one, "Curry" in the red one and
"Pudding" in the brown one.

"Now we'll know which pan is which,"
Dani explained to Izzy. "And if we put
the ingredients in the circles after we've added
them to the right pan, we won't accidentally
use them twice."

Chapter 4

"Great idea!" said Izzy. "That's a clever way to help us keep track when the kitchen is busy."

"It's a shame the spoilt sauces will be wasted, though," stated Asha, about to pour them down the sink. "And the customers who left won't come back."

Dani felt another idea bubbling up.

"Wait!" Dani shouted. "I think I can fix that too!"

She grabbed the chalk pens and raced into the restaurant. When Asha, Tai and Izzy followed Dani, they found her busily scribbling on the menu blackboard.

Dani presented her idea to the whole restaurant with a flourish.

The customers looked excited. The waiter buzzed between tables, taking orders. Asha and Tai were impressed. Izzy looked delighted and Dani was thrilled to have helped.

There were still two empty tables though.

"I know how we can fill those," she thought, picking up the menu board and taking it outside.

Asha and Tai joined Dani outside. Asha held out the pack of chalk pens.

"I'm glad they saved the sauces," said Dani. "You can keep them."

"It's your clever idea that will prevent any future mix-ups, not the chalk pens!" smiled Tai. "You take them, as a souvenir of your adventure."

Today's Special

Lucky Dip Lunch

Sweet and Sour Surprises!

As Dani took the pack from Tai, she felt a tingle in her hand. Then her arm. Then her whole body started spinning and tumbling, away from the restaurant …

Chapter 5

When the spinning stopped, Dani found herself back in the spare bedroom. She put the pack of chalk pens in the toy box and closed the lid.

"What a stirring adventure!" she told her sister Tara. "The chalk pens were vital ingredients, but my cooking circles were the icing on the cake … or the toffee syrup on the pudding!"

Tara smiled. "The toy box has given you a taste for trying things out, Dani," she said. "I wonder what will be on the menu next time?"

How does Dani help with the sauces?

23

Ideas for reading

Written by Clare Dowdall, PhD
Lecturer and Primary Literacy Consultant

Reading objectives:
- discuss the sequence of events in books and how items of information are related
- draw on what they already know or on background information and vocabulary provided by the teacher
- make inferences on the basis of what is being said and done
- predict what might happen on the basis of what has been read so far

Spoken language objectives:
- give well-structured descriptions and explanations
- use spoken language to develop understanding through speculating, hypothesizing, imagining and exploring ideas

Curriculum links: Design technology: Making and evaluating

Interest words: chef, recipes, chalk, bustling, sauce, distracted, vital, ingredients

Resources: salad dressing, golden syrup, curry sauce, etc. for a taste test, paper and pencils

Build a context for reading

- Look at the front cover, read the title, and ask children to describe what they can see in the picture. Develop key vocabulary to describe what Dani is doing, using and wearing.
- Ask children to read the blurb and then suggest what might happen in this story. Challenge them to focus on the clues in the language: *can new chef Dani Binns keep her cool as things heat up in the busy restaurant kitchen?* Discuss what the phrases: *keep her cool; things heat up* might mean in literal and figurative terms.
- Ask children to suggest what it might be like in a restaurant kitchen – based on their experiences visiting restaurants or seeing them on screen.

Understand and apply reading strategies

- Read pp2–3 to the children. Ask them to suggest how the chalk pens might relate to the front cover and the blurb – what might chalk pens be used for in restaurant kitchens?